KEEP HAPPY AND COLOR ON

zendoodle coloring presents

KEEP HAPPY AND COLOR ON

75 delightful designs

WITH PERFORATED PAGES!

ST. MARTIN'S GRIFFIN
NEW YORK

www.stmartins.com

ISBN 978-1-250-09334-9 (trade paperback)

Our books may be purchased in bulk for promotional, educational,
or business use. Please contact your local bookseller or the
Macmillan Corporate and Premium Sales Department at
1-800-221-7945, extension 5442, or by e-mail at
MacmillanSpecialMarkets@macmillan.com.

First Edition: October 2015

10 9 8 7 6 5 4 3 2

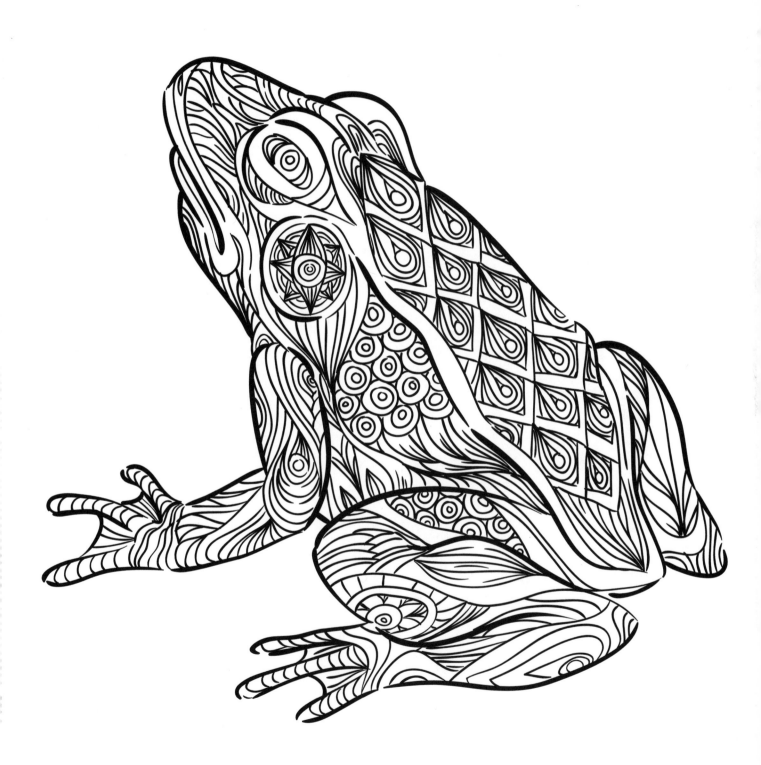

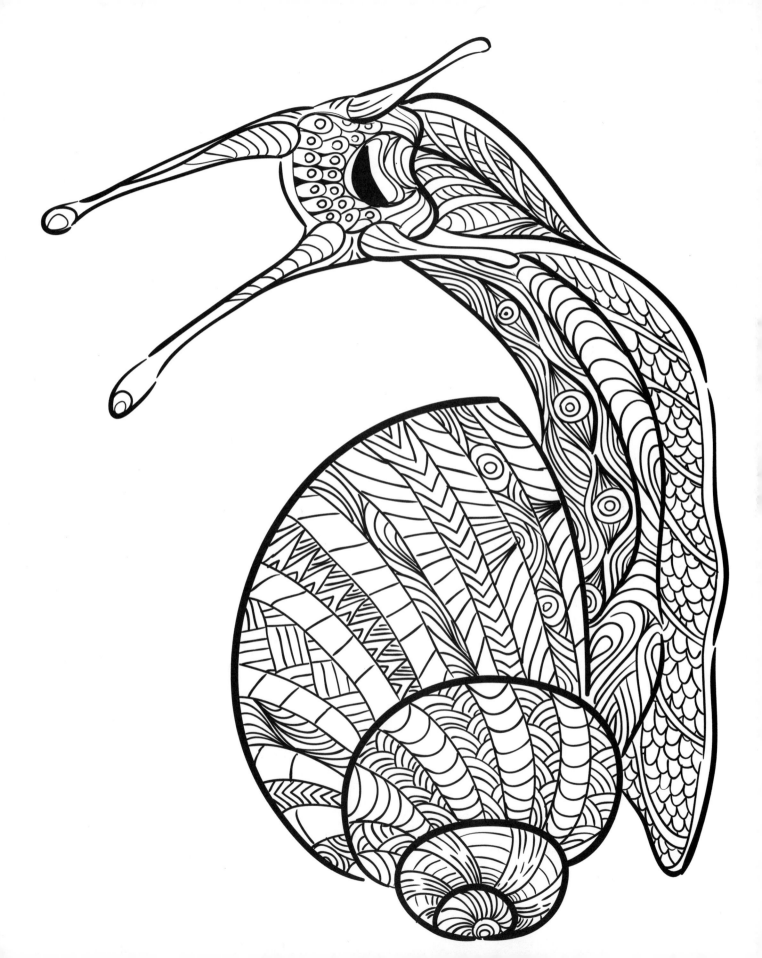

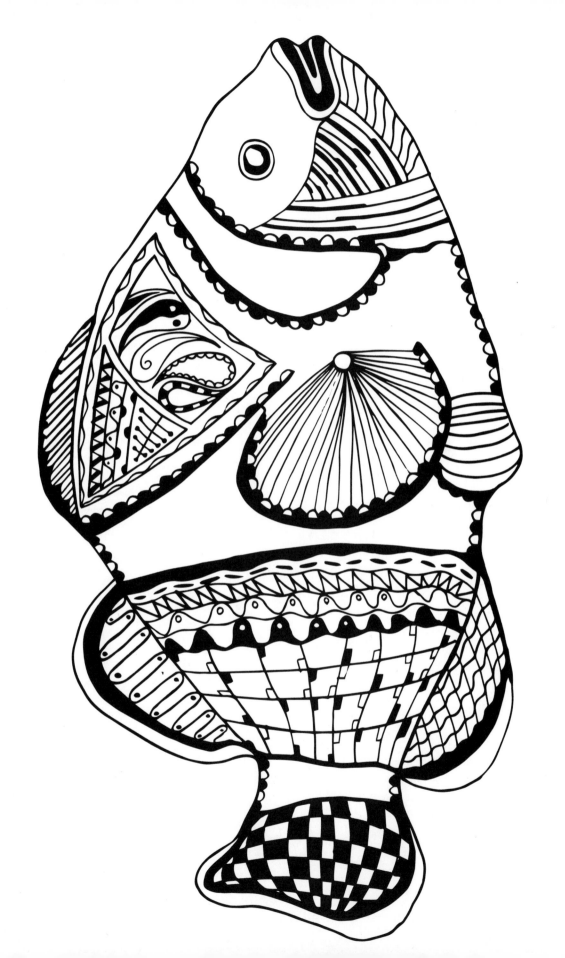

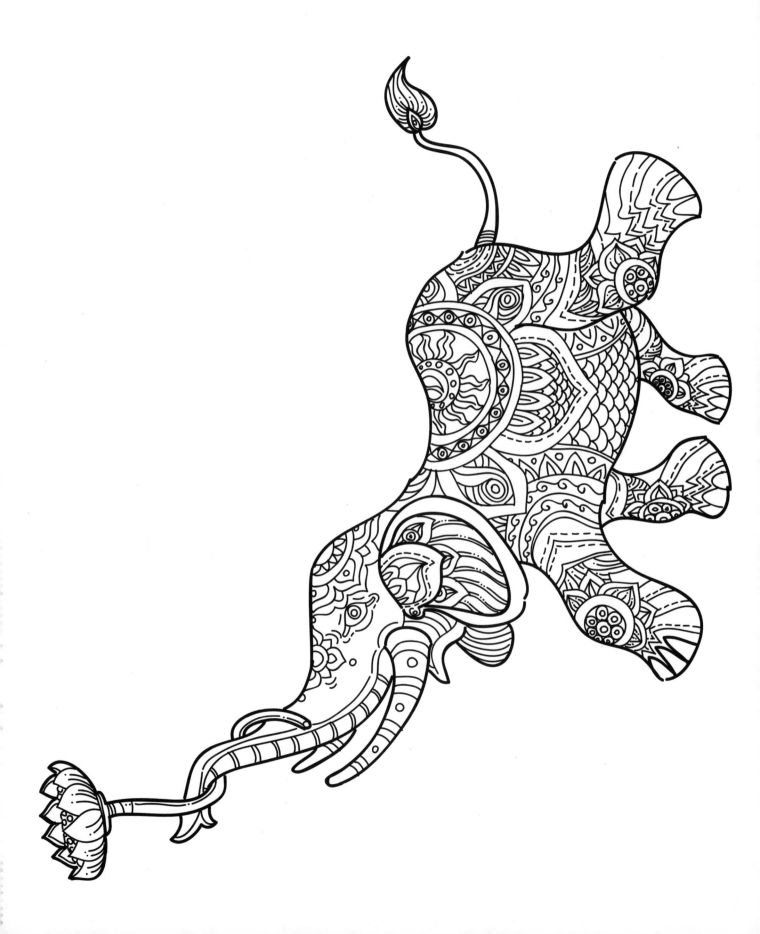

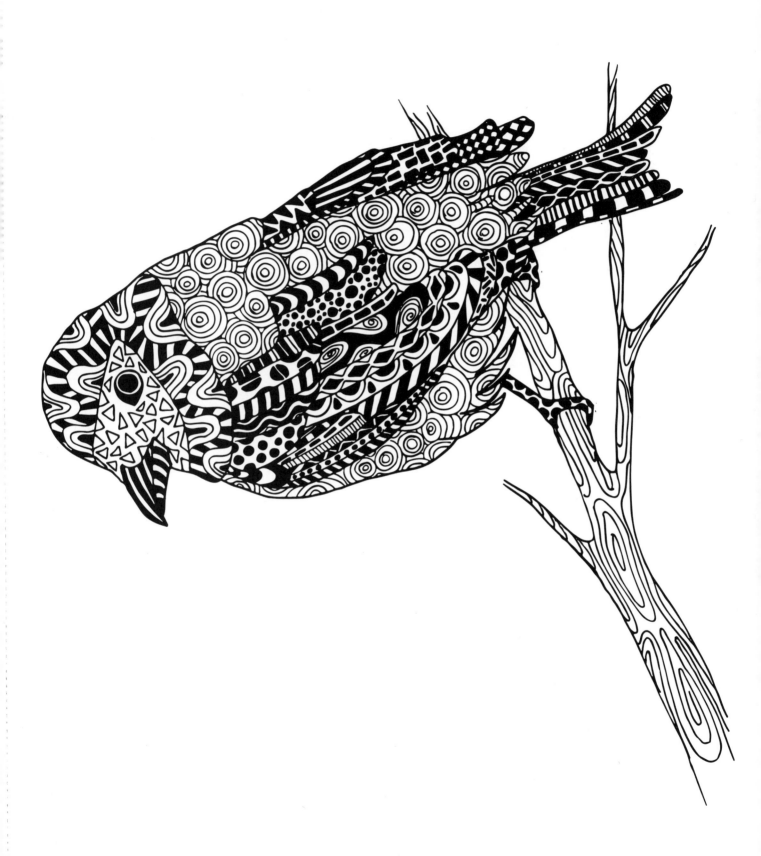

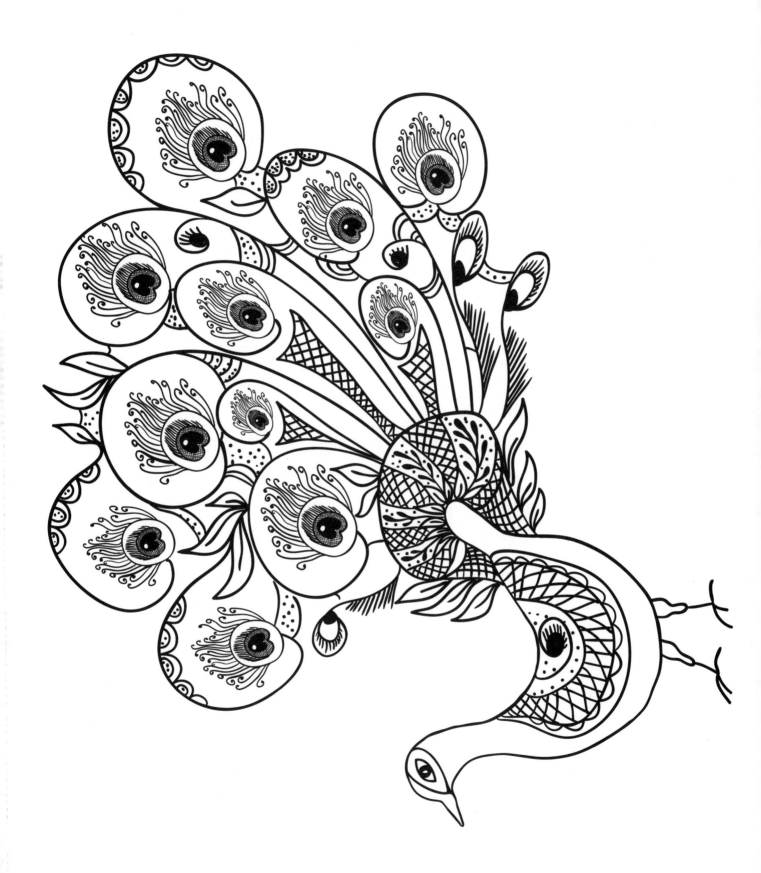

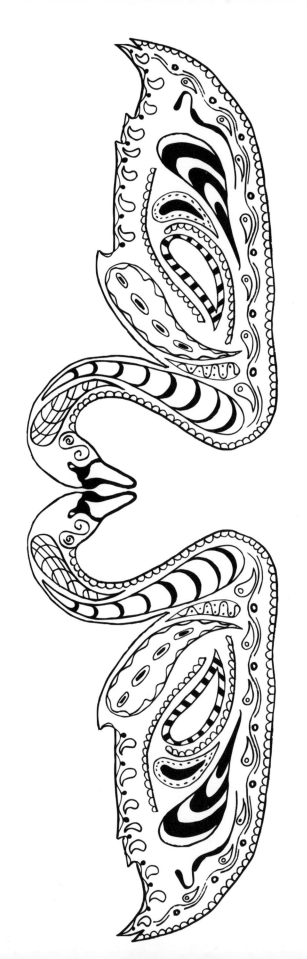

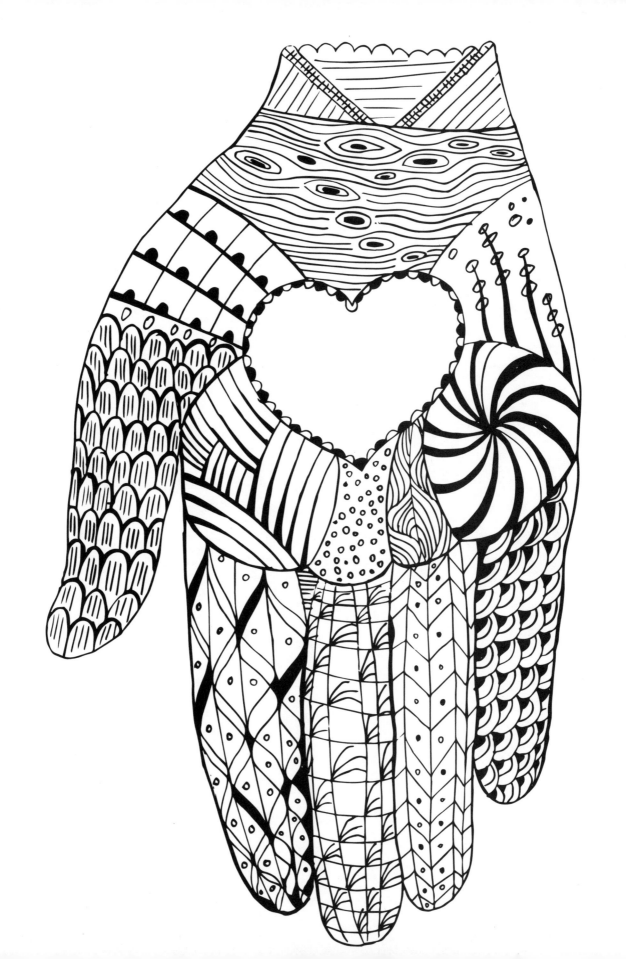

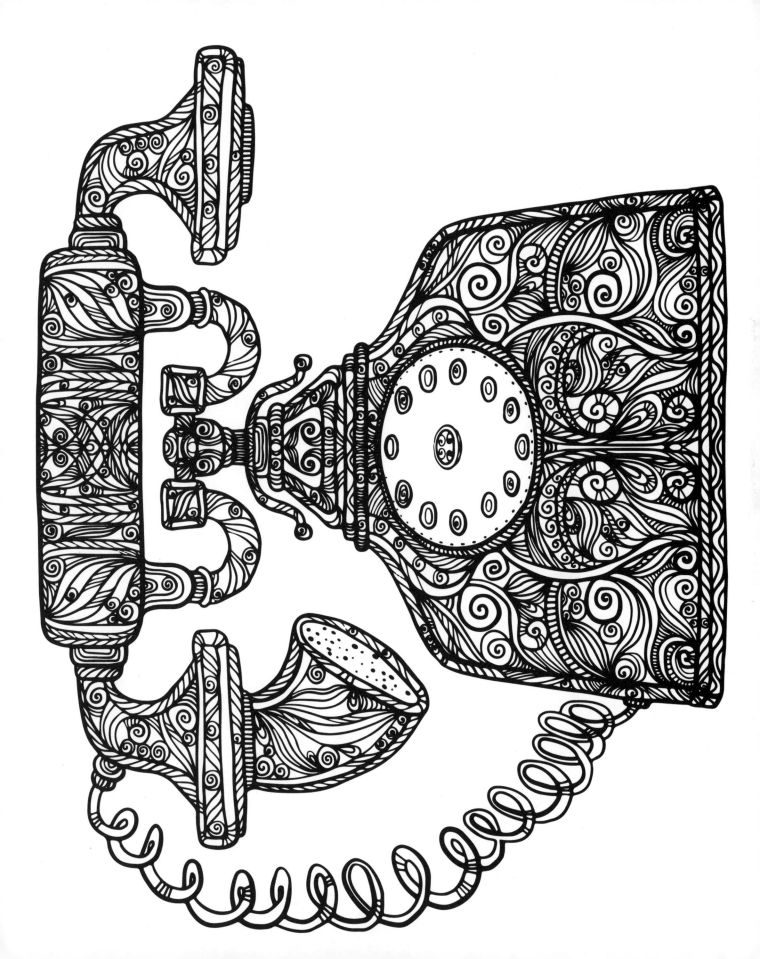

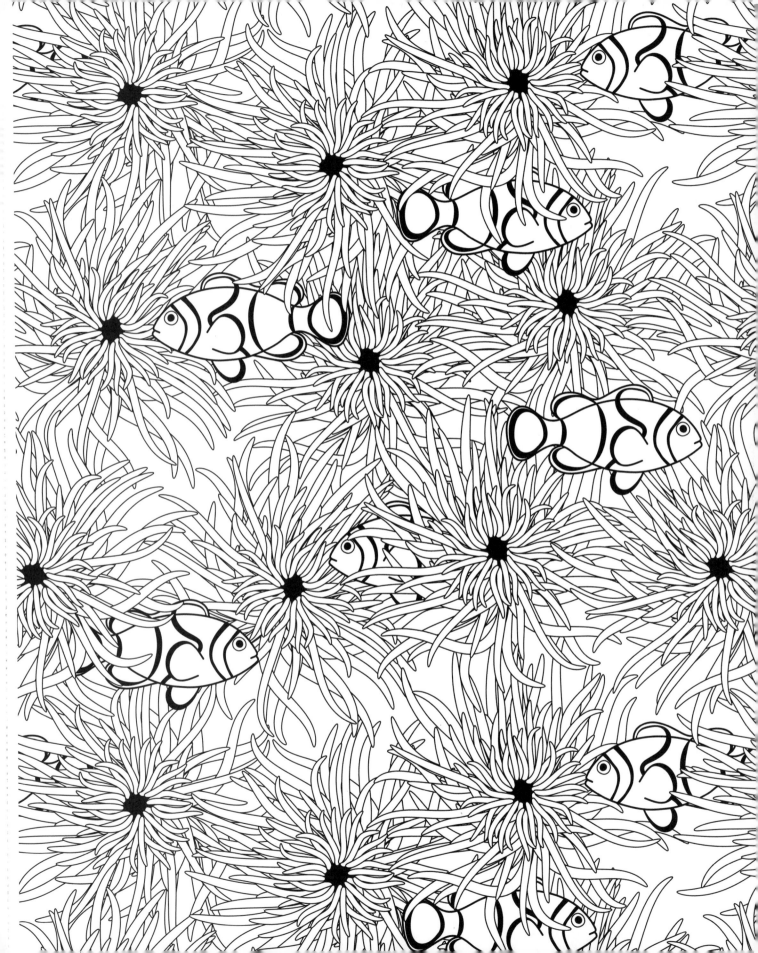